ILLUMINATING MINISTRY

a journal

Victor J. Klimoski, Editor

Saint John's
SCHOOL OF THEOLOGY·SEMINARY
Prepare to Serve

www.csbsju.edu/sot

LITURGICAL PRESS
Collegeville, Minnesota

www.litpress.org

The images contained in *Illuminating Ministry: A Journal* are reproductions of the illuminations found in *The Saint John's Bible.* A monumental achievement and historic undertaking, *The Saint John's Bible* is the only handwritten and illuminated Bible commissioned by a Benedictine Abbey since the advent of the printing press more than five hundred years ago. In the Middle Ages, monasteries helped preserve knowledge and culture for the sake of the greater community. By commissioning a handwritten Bible, Saint John's Abbey and University in Collegeville, Minnesota, revives a tradition and affirms a commitment to the study of Scripture, to the book arts, and to educational, artistic, and spiritual pursuits. *The Saint John's Bible* is a unique blend of ancient methods, materials, and tools with modern themes, images, and technology. It is being made entirely by hand and uses traditional materials including inks, hand-ground pigments, and gold and silver leaf. The renowned calligrapher and illuminator Donald Jackson, in collaboration with scribes, artists, and theologians, directs the creation of *The Saint John's Bible*. When all seven volumes of *The Saint John's Bible* are completed, they will be carefully preserved at the Hill Museum & Manuscript Library at Saint John's University and will be made available as the focus of educational instruction in many forms. Visit www.saintjohnsbible.org to learn more.

This book was edited by Victor J. Klimoski, Director, Lifelong Learning, School of Theology•Seminary, Saint John's University with funding from the Lilly Endowment.

ISBN 978-0-8146-3342-7

CONTENTS

INTRODUCTION

This resource for theological reflection in ministry weaves together tradition and ministerial experience. Each chapter takes as its focus a charism or value in Benedictine spirituality. Some values like hospitality, community, conversatio, and reverence for all persons will be familiar. Others may sound more spiritually generic. That is because Benedict's fundamental belief was that all of life finds its direction in Christian discipleship. The Gospel, not Benedict's particular genius, is the source of any charism associated with a Benedictine vision of life.

In the summer of 2009, the School of Theology•Seminary invited six seasoned pastoral ministers to join Barbara Sutton, director of ministerial formation, to create this journal. Each member of the writing team was assigned a charism and asked to develop a "pastoral instruction" around it. The process began with each person drawing on a ministry experience that captured for the minister the heart of the charism. As their stories unfolded, the ministers then chose an illumination from *The Saint John's Bible* that anchored their stories in the larger story that defines Christian life. Each minister has also written reflections on the text related to the illumination and on the charism as additional resources.

In a way, the stories of the ministers are themselves another type of "illumination." In them, one will discover obvious lessons about Christian life and values. Like an illumination in *The Saint John's Bible*, however, the stories layer in the mysterious encounter and insight these ministers have gained from their practice of ministry. The stories go beyond attempts to simply define how values of Christian discipleship are evident in life. Rather, they are richly textured narratives about how the events of pastoral ministry form, deepen, and extend the minister's understanding of God's continuing revelation.

This resource supports the practice of theological reflection as an essential habit of excellent ministry. The stories invite exploration and stimulate those who read them to retrieve their own stories about the way Christian values find expression in diverse, complex, and unexpected ways. The ministers on the writing team share their insights into how the Scriptures—and the illuminations—influence how they as ministers interpret their pastoral experiences. Finally, while each minister has considered the charism in light of what Benedictine and other scholars have written, the commentaries are personal expressions of how this value connects to pastoral life.

We are grateful to the writing team for the time and efforts they have given to this endeavor, including a three day retreat in Collegeville. Each comes from a demanding life and has responded out of a sense of generosity and responsibility for contributing to the on-going formation of those in ministry. Their wisdom benefits all.

Victor Klimoski
Editor

GROUP SPIRITUAL COMPANIONING

And let us consider how to provoke one another to love and good deeds, not neglecting to meet together, as is the habit of some, but encouraging one another, and all the more as you see the Day approaching. Hebrews 10:24-25

Most people find it helpful to have someone to companion them on their faith journey as they seek to deepen their relationship with God. Such companionship increases our capacity to listen to God in prayer and through one another as we grow in Christian community and in our sense of God's path for us. Spiritual companioning is a process that focuses on conscious development of the relationship between a person and God in either one-to-one (spiritual direction) or small group settings.

Spiritual companioning groups gather to share life experiences, listen to the promptings of God in the stories of others, and explore the call to ministry and the discernment of gifts. At the heart of these gatherings is the opportunity to pray together. Groups also strive to promote an atmosphere of listening and responding to God's voice in daily experiences enkindling our desires to be more fully alive and active in the world and in service to the church. They also provide an opportunity for each person to receive support and challenge from a small community of peers who are listening to and praying for each other.

This spiritual companioning journal is designed for both personal and communal discernment. The prayer movement through this journal is based on *lectio divina*. While there is no standard way to do *lectio*, there are generally six aspects to this spiritual practice:

- **Lectio**/Listening—Listen for God's word or a passage that touches the heart.

• **Meditatio**/Meditating—Ruminate on the word. Allow the word or passage to dwell within you. Allow this pondering to invite you into dialogue with God and then in the spirit of Pentecost, share it with the group.

• **Visio**/Seeing—Return to God's word for the purpose of "hearing and seeing" Christ in the text. Fix your gaze on the illumination. Ask God to open the eyes of your heart, enabling you to see what God wants you to see. Be open to images, thoughts, impressions and feelings that come into your awareness.

• **Oratio**/Speaking—Speak to God. Allow for the transformation of being and feelings. Give to God what you have found in your heart.

• **Contemplatio**/Contemplating—Notice the transforming presence of God within you. Surrender all that is stirring, if only briefly, and rest in God's embrace.

• **Conversatio**/Conversing—Return to God's word. How is your "way of life" impacted by the "seeing and hearing" the word of God today? How does God want you to be different today as a result of this encounter?

This journal invites you to put your story in conversation with God's story as well as the stories of your companions. As you record your thoughts, feelings, and prayers, you will become more attentive to God's movement in your life. Another source of companionship in this journal are the stories of seasoned ecclesial ministers as they illuminate their ministerial experiences. The intersection of these stories—yours, God's, and the ministers—should encourage fruitful conversation. Your challenge will be twofold: to find your voice and to hear the voice of God. This will take some silent time listening to God. Resist the temptation to run away from the silence. This silence should lead you naturally into conversation and your commitment to follow where Christ leads. You will find more than enough inspiration in each session.

The goal is not to cover everything in the journal but to ruminate on its contents and savor that which settles in you. You may find the last two pieces of each chapter, the scriptural reflection and commentary on a Benedictine value, something to take with you for your individual exploration. Let them linger with you.

HOSPITALITY

Story

Something's wrong with this picture, I thought, or rather felt, as my stomach tightened. The assembly consisted almost entirely of white folks, and all the liturgical ministers were white. But scattered around the back of the worship space—and standing in the gathering space—was a sizable number of people of color, seemingly from every part of the globe. Why were they "on the margins" of our assembly?

As parish liturgist I brought my concerns to the liturgy committee. We decided to devote a weekend to recruiting people of color to serve in various liturgical ministries. Our plan was to put cards in the pews for people from other ethnic backgrounds to fill out, noting ministries that interested them. We would then be available after Masses to answer any questions they might have and welcome them with open arms into our liturgical ministries.

That was when the Holy Spirit intervened the first time. I looked around at the liturgy committee and realized that we were all white. I suggested that we actually involve some of "them" in the discernment process. So we invited people of various ethnicities to gather with us to decide together how to move forward.

The first time the liturgy committee met with parishioners from the various ethnic groups, I laid out our solution to the problem expecting grateful kudos from everyone. Instead, I encountered a long, painful silence. Enter the Holy Spirit—a second time. "Our goal is to help everyone feel welcome and at home in our faith community," I ventured. "We need to hear your voices to know if this is a good way to begin." More silence. At last, one brave soul blurted out, "I sit in back because I feel comfortable there. You're asking me to solve your problem. If you really want to welcome me, don't start by asking me to meet your needs. Start by getting to know me as a person and asking how you can meet my needs." One by one, each echoed this response: They still felt like strangers in someone else's home. Other parishioners seemed unable to see past their skin color and clothing to relate to them as individuals. Come, Holy Spirit, fill the hearts of your faithful . . .

A stumbling too-little-too-late apology sputtered from my lips. Another silence. Then, gradually, a new idea emerged from the gathering. We needed to erase the language—and the reality—of *us* and *them*. We needed a weekend when *all* of us could share the richness of our cultures. We needed to help people minister to each other and knit relationships from the strands of ethnic differences. We needed a party.

In what ways does your own experience with hospitality connect with this story?

How does this story shape your vocational call?

What does hearing this story with "the ear of the heart" illuminate in you as you explore the practice of ministry?

Anointing Jesus' Feet
Luke 7:36-50

One of the Pharisees asked Jesus to eat with him, and he went into the Pharisee's house and took his place at the table. And a woman in the city, who was a sinner, having learned that he was eating in the Pharisee's house, brought an alabaster jar of ointment. She stood behind him at his feet, weeping, and began to bathe his feet with her tears and to dry them with her hair. Then she continued kissing his feet and anointing them with the ointment. Now when the Pharisee who had invited him saw it, he said to himself, "If this man were a prophet, he would have known who and what kind of woman this is who is touching him—that she is a sinner." Jesus spoke up and said to him, "Simon, I have something to say to you." "Teacher," he replied, "speak." "A certain creditor had two debtors; one owed five hundred denarii, and the other fifty. When they could not pay, he canceled the debts for both of them. Now which of them will love him more?" Simon answered, "I suppose the one for whom he canceled the greater debt." And Jesus said to him, "You have judged rightly." Then turning toward the woman, he said to Simon, "Do you see this woman? I entered your house; you gave me no water for my feet, but she has bathed my feet with her tears and dried them with her hair. You gave me no kiss, but from the time I came in she has not stopped kissing my feet. You did not anoint my head with oil, but she has anointed my feet with ointment. Therefore, I tell you, her sins, which were many, have been forgiven; hence she has shown great love. But the one to whom little is forgiven, loves little." Then he said to her, "Your sins are forgiven." But those who were at the table with him began to say among themselves, "Who is this who even forgives sins?" And he said to the woman, "Your faith has saved you; go in peace."

were blind. [22] And he answered them, "Go and tell
John what you have seen & heard: the blind receive
their sight, the lame walk, the lepers[m] are cleansed,
the deaf hear, the dead are raised, the poor have
good news brought to them. [23] And blessed is any
24 one who takes no offense at me." When John's
messengers had gone, Jesus[n] began to speak to the
crowds about John[o]: "What did you go out into the
wilderness to look at? A reed shaken by the wind?
[25] What then did you go out to see? Someone[p] dressed
in soft robes? Look, those who put on fine clothing
and live in luxury are in royal palaces. [26] What then
did you go out to see? A prophet? Yes, I tell you, &
more than a prophet. [27] This is the one about whom
it is written,

'See, I am sending my messenger ahead of you,
who will prepare your way before you.'

[28] I tell you, among those born of women no one is
greater than John; yet the least in the kingdom of
God is greater than he." [29] (And all the people who
heard this, including the tax collectors, acknowledged
the justice of God[q], because they had been baptized
with John's baptism. [30] But by refusing to be bap-
tized by him, the Pharisees & the lawyers rejected
31 God's purpose for themselves.) "To what then
will I compare the people of this generation, and
what are they like? [32] They are like children sitting
in the marketplace and calling to one another,

'We played the flute for you, and you did not dance;
we wailed, and you did not weep.'

[33] For John the Baptist has come eating no bread &
drinking no wine, and you say, 'He has a demon';
[34] the Son of Man has come eating & drinking, and
you say, 'Look, a glutton and a drunkard, a friend
of tax collectors and sinners!' [35] Nevertheless, wis-
36 dom is vindicated by all her children." One of the
Pharisees asked Jesus[r] to eat with him, and he went
into the Pharisee's house and took his place at the
table. [37] And a woman in the city, who was a sinner,
having learned that he was eating in the Pharisee's
house, brought an alabaster jar of ointment. [38] She
stood behind him at his feet, weeping, and began to
bathe his feet with her tears and to dry them with
her hair. Then she continued kissing his feet and
anointing them with the ointment. [39] Now when
the Pharisee who had invited him saw it, he said to
himself, "If this man were a prophet, he would have
known who and what kind of woman this is who
is touching him—that she is a sinner." [40] Jesus[t] spoke
up & said to him, "Simon, I have something to say
to you." "Teacher," he replied, "speak." [41] "A certain
creditor had two debtors; one owed five hundred
denarii[s], and the other fifty. [42] When they could not
pay, he canceled the debts for both of them. Now
which of them will love him more?" [43] Simon an-
swered, "I suppose the one for whom he canceled
the greater debt." And Jesus said to him, "You have
judged rightly." [44] Then turning toward the woman,
he said to Simon, "Do you see this woman? I entered
your house; you gave me no water for my feet, but
she has bathed my feet with her tears & dried them
with her hair. [45] You gave me no kiss, but from the
time I came in she has not stopped kissing my feet.
[46] You did not anoint my head with oil, but she has
anointed my feet with ointment. [47] Therefore, I tell
you, her sins, which were many, have been forgiven;
hence she has shown great love. But the one to whom
little is forgiven, loves little." [48] Then he said to her,
"Your sins are forgiven." [49] But those who were at
the table with him began to say among themselves,
"Who is this who even forgives sins?" [50] And he said
to the woman, "Your faith has saved you; go in peace."

YOU GAVE ME NO KISS

m The terms leper and leprosy can refer to several diseases
n Gk he
o Gk him
p Or Why then did you go out? To see someone
q Or praised God
r Gk him
s The denarius was the usual day's wage for a laborer
t Gk he

Scripture Reflection

Brendan Byrne identifies Luke 7:36-50 as a prime example of the movement of God's hospitality that can be seen throughout Luke's gospel. "Jesus, the divine visitor to the world, comes as guest to this house . . . A person . . . on the margins—is drawn to the occasion . . . Boldly, she breaks through the barrier of hostility to herself and her kind. She, not the Pharisee, gives hospitality to Jesus. In return, she receives from him a new outflow of the 'hospitality of God.'"[1] Her great love gives her courage to risk all, and in the end "she carries with her the messianic peace of one transformed by Jesus' power to save."

In the illumination, we see a woman so focused on the presence of Jesus that she can be neither distracted nor dissuaded from expressing her love. She seems unaware of the chaos she has brought to this tidy male gathering, a chaos reflected in the upturned table, the spilled wine and scattered dishes. Simon's ritual cloth attempts without success to maintain the purity and status of both Simon and his guests in the face of her presence. Jesus himself is nowhere to be seen. Yet, a halo-like circle of gold juxtaposed with a dark vertical dividing line suggest a new wholeness and peace that have broken through and become available to those gathered because of the woman's risky act of hospitality.

This gospel passage smashes our nice, neat notion of hospitality. By his half-hearted act of hospitality in inviting this strange man, Jesus, to share his table, Simon has unwittingly opened his door to a divine intervention that upends assumptions about order, status, and purity in his life. The nameless woman who has always been excluded recognizes the presence of God in Jesus. She is the one who truly welcomes him and it will cost her dearly. Her tears may flow as much from regret and loss as they do from love. Now, neither Simon nor the woman will be able to return to their former lives or self-identities. Their future has been changed forever by their encounter with this divine guest. They will need the gift of peace to dwell in the world of messy possibility created by the hospitality of God.

[1] Brendan Byrne, *The Hospitality of God: A Reading of Luke's Gospel* (Collegeville: Liturgical Press, 2000), 75.

What transformation is God inviting you to undergo?

Connecting the Charism

Hospitality

"All guests who present themselves are to be welcomed as Christ, for he himself will say: 'I was a stranger and you welcomed me' (Matthew 25:35)." Rule of St. Benedict 53:1

The Rule of St. Benedict invites us to welcome as though they were Christ the strangers, the poor, and all who present themselves to us. While we may be accustomed to envisioning Christ as the divine host at the banquet of God's love, here Benedict focuses on Christ as the divine stranger, ever knocking, waiting to be welcomed. The hospitality that Benedict describes, like that shown by the woman in the gospel narrative, wells up from those holy moments when we open our hearts in welcome to Christ, who heals our woundedness, reveals our dignity, and fills us with peace. We are then liberated to welcome others and open ourselves to the messy possibilities these sacred visitors may bring into our lives. As Daniel Homan and Lonni Collins comment in *Radical Hospitality*, "Hospitality is born in us when we are well loved by God and others. Hospitality is the overflowing of a heart that has to share what it has received."[2]

How can ecclesial ministers share the hospitality that we have received? Clearly, we are called to be fully present to those with and to whom we minister, open to their needs and gifts. Such hospitality empowers others and models hospitality within our communities. But it is not enough for ecclesial ministers alone to practice hospitality or to organize "hospitality ministries." Theologian Letty Russell reminds us that hospitality is a task for everyone in a congregation. We must lead our communities in developing a culture of hospitality so that all the baptized can embrace their call to welcome the stranger. Russell reminds us, "Hospitality can be understood as solidarity with strangers, a mutual relationship of care and trust in which we share in the struggle for empowerment, dignity, and fullness

[2] Daniel Homan, O.S.B., and Lonni Collins, *Radical Hospitality: Benedict's Way of Love* (Brewster, MA: Paraclete Press, 2002), 20.

of life."[3] Such hospitality includes "the creation of institutional conditions that allow persons to flourish and have a say in the shaping of their lives and communities."[4]

As long as some of us feel unworthy, powerless, or estranged from the church, as long as others hang onto control and self-righteousness, as long as factions exist in our communities, and as long as parishes ignore the homeless at their doors, the church will continue to need ecclesial ministers who will support the people of God to live out their calling to welcome the presence of Christ in the poor and the stranger.

Are you at peace in the world of messy possibilities? What makes peace possible for you?

[3] Letty Russell, *Just Hospitality: God's Welcome in a World of Difference* (Louisville, KY: Westminster John Knox Press, 2009), 20.

[4] Ibid., 122.

COMMUNITY

Story

"Hi. My name is Richard. And I'm an overeater." The meeting of the Overeaters Anonymous group started very mildly. The other five people gathered around a long folding table in the church classroom introduced themselves and their addiction. When it came to my turn, I nervously said my name and explained that I was there to gain insight into addiction and recovery in order to help me become a better minister. I acknowledged the confidentiality of the personal sharing, and the meeting proceeded. At first, I listened intently since I was unfamiliar with the process of addiction support groups. My attention wandered as I felt the exhaustion from my harried day, rushing from one commitment to another and even skipping dinner. I struggled to pull myself back to the present and began jotting a few notes about the meeting's structure to help me stay focused.

One of the members saw me taking notes and was horrified. The group became angry and gravely offended, demanding that I explain myself. I stammered out the reason, but realized that in my eagerness, I had deeply violated their trust. My composure, already stretched thin, suddenly cracked, and I burst into tears, apologized and offered to leave. One woman, Mary, took pity on me and gently asked to know more about me and my purpose before moving forward. The rest of the meeting was brief. I sensed the hesitancy of participants to share with a stranger just listening. Frankly, I didn't blame them. Mary sought me out after the meeting to soothe my feelings, but I was eager to leave and put this disaster behind me.

Later that same evening I gathered with several of my close friends with whom I could lick my wounds and find comfort. Just as we were settling in and opening the wine, an acquaintance of ours stopped by our table and asked if he could join us. I was rather irritated with this interruption because I did not trust him and could not be open with my friends while he was present. My other friends welcomed him to our table as I inwardly cringed. Just as they were pouring him a glass of wine and passing the appetizers, I was shocked into the realization that the tables had been turned. Earlier that evening I had been invited into another community of which I was not a part and had been horrified and deeply embarrassed by my flagrant disrespect of their trust and boundaries. Now this stranger was intruding on my community, and I was acting like we didn't have enough wine, food or friendship to share.

In what ways does your own experience with community connect with this story?

How does this story shape your vocational call?

What does hearing this story with "the ear of the heart" illuminate in you as you explore the practice of ministry?

Life in the Christian Community
Acts 4:32-35

Now the whole group of those who believed were of one heart and soul, and no one claimed private ownership of any possessions, but everything they owned was held in common. With great power the apostles gave their testimony to the resurrection of the Lord Jesus, and great grace was upon them all. There was not a needy person among them, for as many as owned lands or houses sold them and brought the proceeds of what was sold. They laid it at the apostles' feet, and it was distributed to each as any had need.

Life in Community, Aiden Hart with contributions by Donald Jackson, 2002, *The Saint John's Bible*, Hill Museum & Manuscript Library, Order of Saint Benedict, Collegeville, Minnesota, USA.

NOW THE WHOLE GROUP OF THOSE WHO BELIEVED WERE OF ONE HEART AND SOUL
WITH GREAT POWER THE APOSTLES GAVE THEIR TESTIMONY TO THE RESURRECTION OF THE LORD JESUS
I AM
AND NO ONE CLAIMED PRIVATE OWNERSHIP OF ANY POSSESSIONS BUT EVERYTHING THEY OWNED WAS HELD IN COMMON
AND GREAT GRACE WAS UPON THEM ALL
THERE WAS NOT A NEEDY PERSON AMONG THEM

Scripture Reflection

We do not choose the family into which we are born just as we do not choose the people who move in next door to us. And we don't choose who might belong to the same parish. In the eclectic gathering of people we encounter in our various types of communities, we often experience friction and discord. The Acts of the Apostles sets out the ideal community: people of one heart and mind who share all possessions. With this in mind, this illumination might lead us to berate ourselves for not achieving this picture perfect community of the early Christians. We might also question whether this type of community is realistic today. But as we read all of Acts and Paul's letters, we know that the early church encountered challenges of persecution and unbelief as well as conflicts of race and creed. In fact, in this illumination the apostles could just as well be in the midst of a heated argument just as a dense theological discussion.

The icon of the early church community is an invitation to fruitful meditation, not to historical fact. For example, in this illumination we see the apostle Paul alongside Mary and the other apostles, even though Paul's conversion to Christ was not until many years later. There are also additional figures in the circle who represent holy men and women through the ages and around the globe.

In the end, what exactly unites all of the apostles, this ragtag, disparate people, and us? What would motivate us to give up our differences, our possessions, and become one heart and soul? The single purpose and center of all community is Jesus Christ, who is presiding over the gathered in this illumination. He is also the center of the meal that they will share so that they might see Christ and become more like Christ in the breaking of the bread. Authentic community raises our focus above our disagreements or the idiosyncrasies of the person sitting across the table and turns our attention to union in Christ. A community centered on Christ is united in a larger purpose: to live and spread the love of God. Such a community demonstrates its commitment by sharing of self and one's resources and food with each another despite many differences. It may be difficult for us to find anything in common with strangers until by God's grace we recognize Christ in their faces—the same things that happens when we see Christ reflected back to us when we look in a mirror.

The illumination shows that there is always room for another at the table, space to welcome many more members to our community. In similar fashion, the circle is not an end in itself but points to a world beyond it where Christ presides and stands at the margins beckoning us to join him.

Where is your place in this icon?

Connecting the Charism

Community

"Let them prefer nothing whatever to Christ, and may he bring us all together to everlasting life." Rule of St. Benedict 72:11-12

Community is like a circle of people holding up mirrors, reflecting one's true self to each other. They mirror both gifts and areas for growth. People in community speak the truth in love to each other and help them to realize who they fully and really are. They also call forth and refine gifts present among them—perhaps some that people didn't even realize they possessed! Christian community is about each member pouring forth his or her baptismal gifts for the greater good and being filled up by the gifts of others in return. I cannot keep my God-given gifts to myself out of selfishness or doubt of the worthiness of my offering. If I withhold my gifts, there is a hole in the fabric of the community that cannot be filled by another. As I share myself, perhaps there is another who responds to a need of mine. In giving, we learn to be vulnerable and to open ourselves to others. We learn to ask for what we need. We are Christ for one another.

But how do we really "do" community if we don't live in a monastery or even live in one place for more than a few years? The reality is that many ministers and parish priests frequently relocate for a variety of reasons. Weaving an authentic community may become more challenging but has the potential to be richer and deeper by including both long-distance and local friends whom God has placed in our lives. My long-term, long-distance friends listen, encourage and challenge me because of the bonds of trust we have cultivated over the years. Depending entirely upon a long-distance community, however, is not healthy. Our desire for face-to-face contact cannot be fulfilled by an Internet connection. We are body people, and we need other bodies to fulfill a physical and sacramental presence in our lives. So we must build and be community in whatever location God may place us.

That is why being attentive to this idea of gifts is so crucial. We know that ultimately God creates and completes community as a manifestation of God's own Trinitarian life. Through the active sharing of gifts across our differences and our sense of strangeness, grace propels us into new relationships where we discover what it means to be in communion both with those we are easily comfortable and with those often left on the margins.

What gifts do you bring to creating community with others? Where do you withhold these gifts?

LISTENING

Story

When I was ordained for the Diocese of Rapid City in 1981, I was full of life, promise and hope as I embarked on this new journey as a priest. I was excited to put everything that I learned in the seminary—every theory, every idea—into practice. The seminary had been a great experience for me because there was a structure to each day around prayer, worship and study. It was definitely a honeymoon period.

However, the honeymoon didn't last long as I began my pastoral work. Prayer and study were now my responsibility alone. I remember feeling quite disappointed when I was not able to get the other priests I lived with to pray the Liturgy of the Hours with me. One had even reminded me that seminary was over and real life was now upon me.

The frantic pace of parish life began to consume me. Faith formation programs, sacramental preparation, funerals, weddings, committee meetings, and preaching took more and more of my time. Though it was gradual, parish ministry began to swallow me up whole. Over time my prayer life and study begin to slip, and, in the end, I fell into the familiar lie that my ministry was my prayer.

The spark in ministry began to wane as I found myself preaching last minute sermons, trying to affect people second hand, and believing even more that my busyness was my prayer. In summer 2002, my spiritual director had the courage to tell me that I was spiritually dead. He said that God was absent in our conversations and that I had nothing to bring to our sessions. His statement took my breath away. My heart pounded with fury and anger at him. What did he know about prayer? I was so mad that

I didn't speak to him for six months. But in the end I came to see he knew my heart better than I did.

And so I gave my life to Christ again and began the second watch in my ministry, regrouping and starting over again. This time I listened with the ear of my heart, which meant I could not simply talk about prayer anymore, but I had to actually become a person of prayer. I carved out times each day in which I would enter into the silence of my own heart away from e-mails, the phone, and meetings so I could just simply be with the Lord, to allow the Lord to love me, and for me to love the Lord back.

This sort of deep listening that makes privileged room for the Lord each day has changed me. My ministry of presence now is fueled by an intentional daily encounter with Christ and that helps me to attend more deeply to the needs of the people with whom I am called to journey. At the same time, this change has a bite to it because it calls for a level of discipline that cannot be taken for granted or presumed to fit easily within the rhythms of ministerial life. It is about keeping watch and being attentive. It means making choices and changing familiar patterns of life. It confronts the seductive nature of busyness with the question, "Where is the work of Christ in the midst of all this activity?"

In what ways does your own experience with listening connect with this story?

How does this story shape your vocational call?

What does hearing this story with "the ear of the heart" illuminate in you as you explore the practice of ministry?

Sower of the Word
Mark 4:1-9

Again he began to teach beside the sea. Such a very large crowd gathered around him that he got into a boat on the sea and sat there, while the whole crowd was beside the sea on the land. He began to teach them many things in parables, and in his teaching he said to them: "Listen! A sower went out to sow. And as he sowed, some seed fell on the path, and the birds came and ate it up. Other seed fell on rocky ground, where it did not have much soil, and it sprang up quickly, since it had no depth of soil. And when the sun rose, it was scorched; and since it had no root, it withered away. Other seed fell among thorns, and the thorns grew up and choked it, and it yielded no grain. Other seed fell into good soil and brought forth grain, growing up and increasing and yielding thirty and sixty and a hundredfold." And he said, "Let anyone with ears to hear listen!"

to the sea, and
owed him; 8 hear-
e to him in great
dumea, beyond
Tyre and Sidon.
at ready for him
ould not crush
hat all who had
him. 11 Whenever
ell down before
of God!" 12 But
ke him known.
lled to him those
him. 14 And he
amed apostles,[d]
to proclaim the
cast out demons.
on [to whom he
of Zebedee and
m he gave the
hunder]; 18 and
mew, and Mat
of Alphaeus, &
aean, 19 and Judas
n he went home;
ain, so that they
were saying,
nd the scribes
, "He has Beel
ns he casts out
im, and spoke
cast out Satan?
tself, that king

Lectio • Meditatio • Visio • Oratio • Contemplatio • Conversatio

Scripture Reflection

The Parable of the Sower is full of potential for the person who can pay attention—literally: "The one who has ears to hear, let that person hear." To listen with the ear of one's heart is not a passive activity. When we consent to the sowing of the Word in our hearts and receive this seed with openness and joy, we begin to produce yields that are dazzling indeed.

But here is the rub: consenting to the Word of Christ is no easy task. The messiness and complexities of life and ministry become the rocky ground and thorny bushes that crowd, strangle, and scorch what the seed might accomplish in our lives. The illumination for this parable conveys the reality of what happens to the gift of the seed within us when we are consumed with life, relationships and even the work of the Church. When we neglect the depth and richness of the soil within our own hearts, the Word will wither and die for lack of protection and nourishment.

The Parable of the Sower cautions us about everything that fills up our lives. While it is easy to name what is inconsequential in our accumulation of possessions and activities, we are less aware of how the piling on of ministerial work—worthy as it may be—can actually leave no room for the seed to take root and bear its fruit. Without attention to the quality and care of the soil, what is planted will produce a meager harvest at best.

"The one who has ears to hear, let that person hear." We are called in this parable to listen deeply from the center of our being. The consent we give for receiving the Word as Christ's seed in us both expands our own lives and orients us more fully to the world and its needs. This work is not for the faint of heart. It is difficult, demanding and painful at times because, as any farmer or gardener knows, preparing for a good harvest depends on pulling out, digging up, and picking stones—all those things that can compromise the productivity of the soil.

Name those things that prevent the seed of Christ from taking root in your life. How will you respond to the sacred responsibility of preparing the soil for a productive harvest?

Connecting the Charism

Listening

"Listen carefully, my son, to the master's instructions, and attend to them with the ear of your heart." Rule of St. Benedict Prologue: 1

In describing the opening of the Rule of St. Benedict, Esther de Waal uses the image of a crowded marketplace where the Lord is calling out very loudly, trying to get passers-by to stop and listen.[5] For those of us who want to embrace the charism of listening, we first and foremost need to learn the discipline of what it means to "stop" what we are doing and enter into the silence of our hearts where the Lord wants to speak and give to us a revelatory word of hope, promise and new life.

This revelatory word is not a one-time occurrence but happens every day if we simply engage in the practice of listening. Benedict describes listening as more than hearing what is being said and urges us to "listen with the ear of our heart." For one to listen with the ear of one's heart requires, as de Waal points out, appreciating the connection between listening and obedience.[6] The word obedience may run against the grain for many ministers. I know in my own early experience, I misunderstood obedience as something that constricted my ministry and my agenda for parish life and even squelched the movement of the Spirit. But now that misunderstanding of obedience seems to be the consequence of not learning the practice of stopping and listening to the Lord every day. Without this spiritual practice of obedient listening, ministry can easily become overrun by the weeds of one's own desires, leaving no room for the seed of Christ to take root and grow.

Listening comes from the word *obsculta*, to hear, which "involves a reverent, ready, humble way of listening."[7] This demands of oneself a complete surrender to the will of Christ, a surrender that lets go of attachments in life and ministry that prevent us from hearing the voice of the Spirit from within.

[5] Esther de Waal, *Seeking God: The Way of St. Benedict* (Collegeville, MN: Liturgical Press, 1999), 41.

[6] Ibid., 43.

[7] Ibid., 42.

Listening with the ear of the heart means that we are consenting to the voice of Christ, giving Jesus the freedom to bear fruit through us for the sake of the world. Listening means that we are willing to respond without counting the cost of discipleship and to create the interior space where we might discover who we are to become in Christ.

How does the connection between obedience and listening affect your sense of on-going formation for ministry?

REVERENCE FOR ALL PEOPLE

Story

Rooster's eyes were blue. I know this because he let me see deeply into them. They were a distant, glacial blue when angry, but a glistening June-sky blue when smiling. The difference, as for so many of us, was a matter of how Rooster felt others were treating him.

Rooster experienced even little things with mood altering intensity. July suns blazed hotter, March rains drilled deeper, and January winds slapped harsher. In Rooster's world, ice was colder; concrete was harder. I hesitate to call him homeless because, as he taught me, *homeless* is a label. Rooster's home was in the doorways, alleys, parks and streets. And like me, he wanted to be treated with respect and dignity in his own home.

We sat together with nightlife traffic zipping by and he let me in. His stories of Vietnamese jungles, frustrated hopes and a deceased bride were rich, tragic, even comedic at times. They weighed heavily and tired his soul, but they were not the reasons he cried. When his blue eyes faded grey with tears, he was speaking of loneliness and anonymity. Rooster spoke of ripe hurt when people avoided eye contact with him; when pedestrians crossed the street rather than pass him on the sidewalk; when even the do-gooders at the soup kitchen looked past him without speaking.

Prior to sitting with and listening to Rooster, I would have felt for him, sure, but the feeling would have been intellectual, not personal—pity, not compassion. I would have seen him as a statistic, a social problem: evidence of the need to reform our socio-economic institutions. Sadly, I would have been blind to his divine humanness. I would have seen him as having been created in the image and likeness of social injustice rather than in the image and likeness of God.

When it was time to go—I to my home, Rooster to his—he pulled me into a close embrace. Through a pungent cornucopia of diesel exhaust, soiled clothing, human sweat, unwashed hair, un-bathed flesh and whiskey breath, Rooster spoke with a gentle but tear-cracked voice, "Thank you, Steve, for giving me someone to love."

Rooster showed me human sacredness stripped to its naked essence where walls fall and functions crumble, where the subject and object of ministry boil down into the singular soup of God. I drove home changed. Who had just ministered to whom? Who had gifted the other with human reverence and dignity?

Two weeks later a patrolling officer found Rooster's lifeless body on the sidewalk. He radioed dispatch. A team designated to deal with such things arrived. As they removed Rooster from his home, they griped about the outcome of a recent Packers game.

In what ways does your own experience with reverencing all people connect with this story?

How does this story shape your vocational call?

What does hearing this story with "the ear of the heart" illuminate in you as you explore the practice of ministry?

Baptism of Jesus
Mark 1:2-11

As it is written in the prophet Isaiah,

"See, I am sending my messenger ahead of you,
who will prepare your way;
the voice of one crying out in the wilderness:
'Prepare the way of the Lord,
make his paths straight,'"

John the baptizer appeared in the wilderness, proclaiming a baptism of repentance for the forgiveness of sins. And people from the whole Judean countryside and all the people of Jerusalem were going out to him, and were baptized by him in the river Jordan, confessing their sins. Now John was clothed with camel's hair, with a leather belt around his waist, and he ate locusts and wild honey. He proclaimed, "The one who is more powerful than I is coming after me; I am not worthy to stoop down and untie the thong of his sandals. I have baptized you with water; but he will baptize you with the Holy Spirit."

In those days Jesus came from Nazareth of Galilee and was baptized by John in the Jordan. And just as he was coming up out of the water, he saw the heavens torn apart and the Spirit descending like a dove on him. And a voice came from heaven, "You are my Son, the Beloved; with you I am well pleased."

Baptism of Jesus, Donald Jackson, 2002, *The Saint John's Bible* and the Hill Museum & Manuscript Library, Order of Saint Benedict, Collegeville, Minnesota, USA.

Scripture Reflection

If it is true that a person's character is revealed by the company he or she keeps, then such was especially true within ancient Galilee's strict class delineations and rules of social interaction. The picture Mark provides of Jesus at the start of his public ministry gives us a window into what drives Jesus' message and ministry, hopefully inspiring us in our own ministries.

When embarking on his mission, Jesus makes a surprising choice for his first disciples: ragamuffin fishermen. These were not priests, Levites or even Pharisees. Mark gives us nothing to indicate they were even "good" Jews as defined by the Law. They were regular guys: hard-working, sweaty, smelly, weather-beaten fishermen who earned their livings on dangerous waters. They lived up to their elbows in the grit of life every single day. These were the people with whom Jesus would live out his ministry, the people to whom he would ultimately entrust his mission. In a culture where class distinctions were rigid and meant everything, Jesus' choice of disciples offers a radically inclusive demonstration of reverence for all people.

The illumination which sets the stage for this story shows John the Baptist stepping aside and leaving Jesus with the crowd. This is where Jesus' ministry happens, where all ministry really happens—among the people. This image of John the Baptist stepping aside—along with the stories of Simon and Andrew abandoning their nets and James and John leaving their father—tell of a price we must pay for discipleship. Entering into Christ's mission—actually experiencing the reverence he shows for all people regardless of status in life—requires us to let go of our own personal agendas and prejudices.

The artist expresses in brilliant motif what happens when we accept the baptismal call to disregard the judgments and class identities that divide people, allowing us to become one with Jesus and others. The world springs to life in vibrant color, flowers bloom, and the sky seems to explode.

Taken together, the text and the illumination tell a complex, yet concise story. It's the story of recognizing the sacred potential in every single person, of discovering and building God's kingdom amidst the people of the world, and of erupting in joy over the realization that each of us—regardless of who we are and what we do—can have an immediate and personal relationship with Jesus.

What is God asking you to surrender before you are able to enter fully into Christ's mission? What price will you pay for discipleship?

Connecting the Charism

Reverence for All People

"He must show every care and concern for the sick, children, guests, and the poor, knowing for certain that he will be accountable for all of them on the day of judgment." Rule of St. Benedict 31:9

Father Dave Beaudry stood in front of our sacramental theology class and implored the group of aspiring ministers not to place him on a pedestal. A few students objected, one rather vehemently, "But you're a priest and I rightly respect you and revere you for that. So even if you don't want to be placed on a pedestal, I still look up to you and hold you in higher esteem than the average Joe."

Shaking his head, Fr. Dave rebuked the deacon candidate, "Listen to yourself. If you hold me or anyone else in higher esteem, you must consequently hold other people in lower esteem. That's the problem." Indeed, that is the problem as well as the challenge. When we speak of reverence for all people, we're speaking of two absolutes: *reverence* and *all people*. This Benedictine value makes no provisions for degrees of reverence or for classifications of people.

This presents us with a spiritual and emotional paradox to say the least. Our natural tendencies lead us to respect attitudes and behaviors which align with our own senses of righteousness and, conversely, to disrespect attitudes and behaviors which are contrary. On the surface, this seems perfectly appropriate. We hate the sin but love the sinner. In practice, however, we are seldom able to separate the person from the actions or attitudes that define his or her life's journey. So when we judge a person's actions—a corporate leader who cheats shareholders, an elected official caught in adultery, a local drunk driver who causes a fatal accident—we inevitably perforate the *faux* line separating the individual and the journey. In disdaining the activity or the motive, we find ourselves diminishing our respect for the person.

The Rule of St. Benedict helps us along by reminding us that each person and each person's journey are sacred. No exceptions. All people are created in the image and likeness of God, thereby created in love, by love, to love and for love. Moreover, each person has the very real potential to reveal that personal and intimate image of God to us. This is true regardless of the person's place along life's journey at any given moment. The Rule asks us to openly accept people as they individually are and where they are on the road, fully recognizing that every individual must discover and grow into holiness in his or her own time and in his or her own way.

In living out reverence for all people, we affirm their sacred destinies, we respect their personal journeys, we lavish them with forgiveness, and we refrain from burdening them with our judgments.

What part of this story triggers the strongest reaction in you? How do these feelings help or hinder your reverence of all people?

JUSTICE

Story

It was dinner time at the Cardinal Manning Center in Los Angeles. Homeless men who had come off the streets of Skid Row to shower and have their dinner filled the day room. With them were my nine college students on an alternative spring break trip. We would spend the evening with these men who would later return to sleep on the sidewalk. Many of these central Minnesota students had never experienced anything like this, but service-learning experiences were part of my work as a campus minister.

As a good leader I knew that I would need to encourage conversation so I asked to join two of the Center's guests as they silently ate their hot dogs and chips. One of the men said nothing, and the other nodded for me to sit. I began to make small talk. One of the men changed tables immediately, and Charles stayed but said nothing. As an experienced minister, sparking conversation was something I knew well so I smiled and continued. "There is nothing better than a good hotdog," I said though I hate hotdogs. There was no reply. "Do you come here often?" Again, no reply. Well, maybe showing how to sit in respectful silence would be a good example for my students who were watching me closely.

After a short time, Charles, looking down at his food, said, "Come outside with me. I want to show you what it's like." My heart sank, and all I could feel was fear—of the dark unlit street, of drug dealers, of pimps, of people suffering with mental illness. Ideals of Christian love were replaced by fear of Charles and what he would show me about his world. I thought quickly and said that I couldn't leave my students. "They will be fine," he said pointing to the staff person at the front desk. Realizing my excuses weren't working, I decided that I just needed to be honest and tell Charles of my fear. "I am too afraid to go out there," I explained hoping that my honesty surely would end his insistence. "I will make sure you are safe," he said. "Nothing will happen. I swear you will be safe with me." He persisted no matter what I said. Over and over in my mind I tried to convince myself to go with him but in the end it was clear to me I could not go so I sat up tall in my chair and said firmly, "Charles, I don't want to go out there." He shouted back at me, "Then I shouldn't have to go out there either!"

In what ways does your own experience with justice connect with this story?

How does this story shape your vocational call?

What does hearing this story with "the ear of the heart" illuminate in you as you explore the practice of ministry?

A PRIEST PASSED BY ON THE OTHER SIDE
A LEVITE PASSED BY ON THE OTHER SIDE
BUT A SAMARITAN WAS MOVED TO PITY
AND BANDAGED HIS WOUNDS
WHICH ONE OF THESE WAS A NEIGHBOR TO THE MAN WHO FELL INTO THE HANDS OF ROBBERS?
אברהם

The Good Samaritan
Luke 10:29–37

But wanting to justify himself, he asked Jesus, "And who is my neighbor?" Jesus replied, "A man was going down from Jerusalem to Jericho, and fell into the hands of robbers, who stripped him, beat him, and went away, leaving him half dead. Now by chance a priest was going down that road; and when he saw him, he passed by on the other side. So likewise a Levite, when he came to the place and saw him, passed by on the other side. But a Samaritan while traveling came near him; and when he saw him, he was moved with pity. He went to him and bandaged his wounds, having poured oil and wine on them. Then he put him on his own animal, brought him to an inn, and took care of him. The next day he took out two denarii, gave them to the innkeeper, and said, 'Take care of him; and when I come back, I will repay you whatever more you spend.' Which of these three, do you think, was a neighbor to the man who fell into the hands of the robbers?" He said, "The one who showed him mercy." Jesus said to him, "Go and do likewise."

Luke Anthology, Donald Jackson with contribution by Aidan Hart and Sally Mae Joseph, 2002, *The Saint John's Bible* and the Hill Museum & Manuscript Library, Order of Saint Benedict, Collegeville, Minnesota, USA.

Scripture Reflection

Looking at the entire illumination, we are drawn in by the color and figures in the accompanying panels while the center panel draws us in by what is not present. There are no figures, only words that will haunt us if we let them. We ask, "Who is our neighbor?" and see no one. Does this suggest that we need to look deeper into our own lives to find her? Regularly in our world we make invisible those persons who are pushed to the margins of our society by gender, poverty, mental illness, race, sexual orientation or social class. Are they the ones we are encouraged to see?

Charles was my "bleeding and naked" man. He wanted to open my eyes to my neighbors and their living conditions, but I resisted seeing. I preferred to be safe behind the doors of the Center. I wanted to have a simple and friendly conversation with him that night, and instead he asked me to cross over into his world. I refused. I didn't want to acknowledge it as part of my ministry. My ministry was to be with the students, guiding them through a learning experience. I had a job to do, and Charles was messing up my neat schedule. I walked by him just like the Levite and the priest for a lot of the same reasons they did. I didn't want to see my neighbors, much less love them.

That night in Los Angeles I chose to make invisible the people whose lives were spent on the streets, and I convinced myself it was the only smart thing to do. That conclusion held until my new teacher told me otherwise. In my life I have had many professional teachers, but in the Cardinal Manning Center, Charles became an unforgettable teacher. Why should he have to go out there every night while I could choose or refuse to have a guided tour? Perhaps like the followers of Jesus who heard this parable, I experienced the discomfort of having to re-think my definition of who really was my neighbor and whether my willingness to "see" my neighbor was conditioned by a wide range of factors. Justice calls for relationships without conditions and relationships that come at a cost. I understood that in a new way as Charles turned and moved to the door—and the street beyond.

What new thresholds are you called to cross? What demand will it make on you?

Connecting the Charism

Justice

"Seek first the kingdom of God and his justice, and all these things will be given you as well (Matt 6:33)." Rule of St. Benedict 2:35

Charity is wonderful, but justice makes people nervous. Why is that? When people are asked to give money or time to local charities, it seems that they are more accommodating. When the word "justice" comes into play, these same people become hesitant and even angry. It would seem that justice asks more, calls individuals to go deeper, and requires a greater investment and even sacrifice on the neighbor's behalf. In a culture of rugged individualism and the image of pulling oneself up by one's boot straps, the idea of sharing what we have and working for the common good requires a kind of compassion that some see as naïve and even dangerous.

The parable of the Good Samaritan, however, gives us an example of what charity moving to justice in action looks like. The hero in this parable was a marginalized member of society and a most unlikely teacher, especially for Jesus' listeners. The Samaritan does not pass by the naked and bleeding victim but instead chooses to help a perfect stranger in circumstances that might even be dangerous. Moved by compassion he stops his life to give the stranger what is needed. The Samaritan chose to get himself dirty as he carried and cleaned the stranger. Certainly that should have been enough, but the stranger needed help beyond binding up his wounds so that he could get back on his feet again. The money and the promise to return proved that the Samaritan had crossed over to the side of the wounded as he moved from charity to justice.

Justice calls us to render to each what is due and also to go deeper and look at the structures and systems that create injustice in the first place. Justice moves us to ask why—why the man was wounded and naked, why others in the community simply passed by, why people like Charles have to go back into the merciless streets, why the divide between the haves and have-nots seems simply a part of life? Justice challenges our own sense of privilege and recognizes the sin that keeps people like Charles living on the margins and invisible. It also challenges us to acknowledge that we can be deceived by our own professed ideals if they are not followed up by action. We must not forget that behind our verbal support for "the issues" are people with names and lives and histories that beg us not to pass them by.

What inner resources do you need to facilitate the difficult conversations around "Why injustice exists?" What moves you beyond verbal support?

STEWARDSHIP

Story

Upon graduation from college, I decided not to attend medical school but instead to serve one year as a lay missionary in the Anawim Community in the Appalachian foothills of southern Ohio. I had met the community a year earlier when I chaperoned a school service trip and was intrigued by these urbanites who pledged to live simply among the rural people they served. We decided I would live as the sole Catholic resident in the little town of Otway (population 198), occupying the empty house next to the church. All the volunteers met for evening meals on the Anawim farm where we took turns cooking vegetarian dishes. My stipend was $100 a month, and my primary task was to help a group of women run a St. Vincent de Paul store. In my seatless cargo van, I would make regular trips to Columbus for donated goods and run deliveries of food and clothes into the hollers when we learned of a family in need. Frequently, I was unnerved by how many people in the area lacked running water, electricity, and formal education.

As the year wore on, I became increasingly frustrated with the inordinate amount of time I spent driving all over the countryside lending and borrowing things. One early spring day, two of us drove to a neighboring village in order to trade three shovels for the use of a breeding goat and two gallons of raw milk. It took us more than half the day. On the return trip eight days later, I eased my goat laden van into another 15 miles per hour S-curve and leaned toward my companion Rita, "Do we really *need* to do all this running around trading stuff?" She noted the irritation in my voice and said smiling, "No, we don't, but it's the Appalachian way. This way, people can have the satisfaction of owning some things but don't need to own all the things. They learn to trust and rely on each other by sharing tools and caring for each others' property. Did you notice how shiny and sharp the axe-head was when John returned it the other day? It's like a co-op: we are interdependent. And, it's no accident that we always end up talking over a cup of tea on the porch. It helps the world seem friendlier, don't you think?"

I couldn't answer because, honestly, I didn't get it. I had come from a world of private-ownership where heated arguments in college over the messiness of the dorm room and the four malt beverages missing from the fridge were the passions of the day. We didn't really share things; we just consumed them in common. Aspects of my life appeared to be pretty superficial in southern Ohio. My initial thought was to blame my discomfort on their "poverty-infused backwoods" lifestyle, but my spirit was not content with so easy an interpretation. Here I was surrounded by people for whom the notion of sharing goods in common was as natural as breathing and where my frustration over the lack of efficiency ran headlong into the primacy of relationships. My perspective on normalcy was blown wide open. Maybe these people, outside the limelight of modern society, were the norm, and perhaps for the first time I was outside looking in.

In what ways does your own experience with stewardship connect with this story?

How does this story shape your vocational call?

What does hearing this story with "the ear of the heart" illuminate in you as you explore the practice of ministry?

Creation Story
Genesis 1:26–2:2

Then God said, "Let us make humankind in our image, according to our likeness; and let them have dominion over the fish of the sea, and over the birds of the air, and over the cattle, and over all the wild animals of the earth, and over every creeping thing that creeps upon the earth."

So God created humankind in his image,
in the image of God he created them;
male and female he created them.

God blessed them, and God said to them, "Be fruitful and multiply, and fill the earth and subdue it; and have dominion over the fish of the sea and over the birds of the air and over every living thing that moves upon the earth." God said, "See, I have given you every plant yielding seed that is upon the face of all the earth, and every tree with seed in its fruit; you shall have them for food. And to every beast of the earth, and to every bird of the air, and to everything that creeps on the earth, everything that has the breath of life, I have given every green plant for food." And it was so. God saw everything that he had made, and indeed, it was very good. And there was evening and there was morning, the sixth day.

Thus the heavens and the earth were finished, and all their multitude. And on the seventh day God finished the work that he had done, and he rested on the seventh day from all the work that he had done.

Creation, Donald Jackson, Donald Jackson with contribution by Chris Tomlin, 2002, *The Saint John's Bible* and the Hill Museum & Manuscript Library, Order of Saint Benedict, Collegeville, Minnesota, USA.

תהו
ובהו

Scripture Reflection

All that exists is present in the first panel of the illumination. Though formless and void of order (the Hebrew words "*tohu wabohu*"), matter explodes outward as if driven by a powerful force. God's red and gold breath, *RUAH*, wrestles the portions of matter into the universe that lulls us to sleep and awakens us each day. A streak of gold light races through the primordial mist hinting of an eternity of Pentecosts. Loving God is active in creation, and it is good.

In the sixth panel, humans (*adam*) are placed in creation to have dominion over it. Since humans are made in the image and likeness of God who is love (1 John 4), their mission is to care for creation in God's stead. This requires reflectivity and an awareness of "the other," something that truly sets us apart within the world. Still, the matter that makes up the human body is present in different forms in each panel. All of creation is intimately interconnected. We are animated with the breath of God, and our destiny is to return to God through mortal death in order to be eternally animated with creation.

God spent "five days" creating a space in which humankind could become fully "actualized." God wanted humans to revel in the Garden and in love. The snake/serpent in the bottom of the sixth panel reminds us that other voices sometimes lead us away from resting in God. All of the human figures are facing away from the seventh panel, perhaps indicative of our tendency to be busy and distracted.

The small gold boxes that increase in number from left to right mark the days, serve as hinges between the panels, and indicate God's presence in the creative process. The geometrical progression of the boxes indicates that God brings order to the chaos of matter, which then exists together. In panel seven where "God rests," we can see more jumbled gold boxes "*in potentia*," awaiting their place in the diverse order of creation.

Imagine living in the white space to the right of the seventh panel—an eighth undrawn panel if you will. The gold boxes serve a cardinal position holding in tension the story of God's previous creation and the imagined potential as God continues to create, order, and animate.

The raven of wisdom present with God in the beginning points to the eighth panel, soaring over creation throughout time. In her shadow, we are called to accept the loving relationship offered to us by God and to treat all creation with reverence since it truly belongs to the creator.

What untapped potential are you holding onto? How would the world be different if this potential were released? How would it affect your relationship with God?

Connecting the Charism

Stewardship

"He will regard all utensils and goods of the monastery as sacred vessels of the altar, aware that nothing is to be neglected." Rule of St. Benedict 31:10–11

Stewardship is rooted in a sacramental view of the world where everything reveals the Creator. For this reason, we are called to revere all that God has made. None of us truly owns anything. Nothing in the created world has more inherent value than any other thing. What a freeing concept: to know that our ultimate satisfaction is not found in "things" themselves but in the relationships that exists between them, us, and the loving Creator.

Stewardship expresses a posture towards life. It is not a popular notion in Western culture that seems to prize material possessions, larger than life personalities, and distracting recreational activities above simplicity, humility, sharing, and honest labor. Even in our worship communities, people pulling together for the common good is often the exception, not the norm. In large, urban parishes, people complain that they do not know the people praying next to them week to week: "Coming to church just feels like more of the same. I don't really feel connected."

An authentic sense of community suffers from people's hesitation to share their time and energy in the face of busy lives. We know that to be a fact. Sometimes change happens in small ways. For example, to encourage greater ownership for the overall good of the community, some parishes form crews of parishioners to regularly clean the common spaces—something often hired out. This simple, mundane task cultivates community relationships as people take responsibility for what they use in common. It is a way in which people are forming a sense of connectedness to one another and to the place where they gather for worship. Without such opportunities, we should not be surprised when people seem indifferent to the dynamics involved in community-making.

"Potlucks are an aspect of stewardship and an experience of communion," I said over my shoulder to the young colleague shuffling through the funeral luncheon line with me. He was picking his way through the dishes, wrinkling his nose at a three-bean salad and grimacing over another bowl of mayonnaised pasta. Shaking his head he whispered, "I despise potlucks. Yuck, cottage cheese in Jell-O! You don't know who or how they made these." "That's exactly the point," I responded. "Someone took the time to make this dish. She generously brought it here for the sake of others. Labor was shared by many people, and there is plentiful food. Now we get to be fed."

How does your understanding of stewardship affect the decisions you make?

CONVERSATIO

Story

When I went to West Virginia to lead the diocesan charge on ministry formation, I was excited, imagining how my gifts would build vibrant parish life. I didn't quite know where to begin. Appalachia was a new context for me. The Appalachian Bishops Pastoral Letter, *This Land Is Home to Me*, should have alerted me about the culture. In it, they wrote: "We must continually take time and invest creatively in listening to the people, especially the poor. The people themselves must shape their own destiny."[8]

Nonetheless, I began by designing a program and gathering people in different areas to get feedback. They were quick to tell me how to make it work so I felt good—I had listened to the people, taken their suggestions and adjusted an adult faith formation program that would surely educate for the gospel's mission. I was ready to take the program on the road.

For my first class in one of the small towns, I met my new students and was received with West Virginia hospitality at its best. Confidently, I gave the group a focus question to discuss at their tables. When asked to share aloud, they told story after story. As I drove home, I wondered when I would make up the content we didn't cover. The following week I limited the focus question, asking them to share only with the person next to them. When I invited summaries, the stories began again. Silently I wondered, "Don't they understand the assignment? Don't they want to learn from me?" After all, I had spent years studying and preparing to do exactly this—give them the knowledge they needed to be faithful disciples!

[8] Appalachian Catholic Bishops, *This Land Is Home to Me: A Pastoral Letter on Powerlessness in Appalachia* (Catholic Committee on Appalachia, 1975), 30.

It became apparent to me, finally, that success wasn't simply having the expertise, using the latest resources, or creating dazzling PowerPoints. What if the lessons to be learned were in the very stories people told? What if my role was to pay attention to the storytelling, drawing upon the people's own wisdom when space opened for teachable moments related to lessons about discipleship, mission, and witness?

This insight changed my approach but not without a struggle. I had come to believe that knowledge was power and that my responsibility was to be the expert. But in these small rural communities, I was being called to surrender my knowledge and empower the wisdom of the community. Their context, shared experience, and history were important "texts" for any learning that would occur. I had been changed by the process and so had the participants. As they wove together their stories of church and family into God's story, they grew in confidence and the dreams of a new community emerged. They had leveled the playing field and each person, including myself, became teacher and learner.

In what ways does your own experience with good conversations connect with this story?

How does this story shape your vocational call?

What does hearing this story with "the ear of the heart" illuminate in you as you explore the practice of ministry?

The Road to Emmaus
Luke 24:13-32

Now on that same day two of them were going to a village called Emmaus, about seven miles from Jerusalem, and talking with each other about all these things that had happened. While they were talking and discussing, Jesus himself came near and went with them, but their eyes were kept from recognizing him. And he said to them, "What are you discussing with each other while you walk along?" They stood still, looking sad. Then one of them, whose name was Cleopas, answered him, "Are you the only stranger in Jerusalem who does not know the things that have taken place there in these days?" He asked them, "What things?" They replied, "The things about Jesus of Nazareth, who was a prophet mighty in deed and word before God and all the people, and how our chief priests and leaders handed him over to be condemned to death and crucified him. But we had hoped that he was the one to redeem Israel. Yes, and besides all this, it is now the third day since these things took place. Moreover, some women of our group astounded us. They were at the tomb early this morning, and when they did not find his body there, they came back and told us that they had indeed seen a vision of angels who said that he was alive. Some of those who were with us went to the tomb and found it just as the women had said; but they did not see him." Then he said to them, "Oh, how foolish you are, and how slow of heart to believe all that the prophets have declared! Was it not necessary that the Messiah should suffer these things and then enter into his glory?" Then beginning with Moses and all the prophets, he interpreted to them the things about himself in all the scriptures.

As they came near the village to which they were going, he walked ahead as if he were going on. But they urged him strongly, saying, "Stay with us, because it is almost evening and the day is now nearly over." So he went

Road to Emmaus, Donald Jackson, 2002, *The Saint John's Bible* and the Hill Museum & Manuscript Library, Order of Saint Benedict, Collegeville, Minnesota, USA.

JESUS HIMSELF CAME NEAR
AND WENT WITH THEM
HE TOOK BREAD, BLESSED &
BROKE IT, & GAVE IT TO THEM:
THEN THEIR EYES WERE OPENED,
AND THEY RECOGNIZED HIM;
AND HE VANISHED
FROM THEIR SIGHT.

in to stay with them. When he was at the table with them, he took bread, blessed and broke it, and gave it to them. Then their eyes were opened, and they recognized him; and he vanished from their sight. They said to each other, "Were not our hearts burning within us while he was talking to us on the road, while he was opening the scriptures to us?"

Scripture Reflection

Without an agenda or a lesson plan, Jesus drew closely to the disciples and asked, "What are you discussing?" He simply walked beside the two disciples on their journey, conversing and listening attentively as they spoke of their joys and anxieties. In time the disciples caught a glimpse into the heart of God and found their world made new. Their hearts were burning! The road opened before them, and they begin to grasp the height and depth of God's mysterious love. Jesus yielded to their readiness.

What draws me into this gospel story is not *where* the two disciples were going, but that they were going *away* from the community of Jesus' disciples in Jerusalem, the place where their hope was sustained, if only briefly. Only seven miles into the trip and they had already become disillusioned and were grumbling. How did they become so emptied of resurrection life?

We can be absorbed by the present, unable to see into the future and its possibilities. Overwhelmed by deadlines, openness to the Spirit and conversion to authentic discipleship become objectified and turn into a destination or one more task. "Destination theology" leaves us fatigued and sometimes reconciled to simply surviving. It does not provide the space to recognize all that God has done in our lives. If left to our own devices, we begin to think that our ability to complete a checklist of things to-do is a significant benchmark for discipleship.

This Emmaus story reminds us of the power of the present to capture our attention and to bury our hope without an eye to the future. Absorbed by daily life, we easily forget the past with its salutary lessons and neglect the future with its rightful claims. We need the stranger and the prophet to startle us and to help us see beyond the present. As tempting as it may be to surrender to disillusionment, we need to attend to the voice of hope.

Like the two disciples on the road to Emmaus or the seventy-two sent on mission, we find our sustaining nourishment in the word of God. We need as well companions who call attention to what seems to block the Spirit's movement. Companions that listen intently as we pour out our story, helping us as Christ did on the Road to Emmaus to see beyond the moment to God's mysterious plan.

In your journey, what connections sustain you for the long-haul?

Connecting the Charism

Conversatio

"If a disciple obeys grudgingly and grumbles, not only aloud but also in his heart, then, even though he carries out the order, his actions will not be accepted with favor by God , who sees that he is grumbling in his heart." Rule of St. Benedict 5:17-18

The synod process was ending as I was beginning my ministry in West Virginia. Bishop Bernard Schmitt led this initiative with an emphasis on the communitarian character of church life. He charged me "to keep my ear to the ground" to hear what people were talking about. He knew inherently that listening would harness the experience and knowledge of people at the grassroots.

The people of West Virginia are strong and rugged individuals who often have little respect or time for people who have all the answers or know best how things should be done for them. They resent it when outsiders think they can impose their ideas on rural folks. They often quip that if outsiders would just ask, they could tell them how to tackle a community problem. After all, they have lived in West Virginia all their life. Imagine their delight when diocesan leaders asked, "What do you ask of the Church?" It came natural for them to sit and talk about the church, giving their point of view, telling it like it is—what would work and what wouldn't. As a result, decisions were made with the participation of the whole diocesan community.

Creating a sustained conversation provided threads needed for re-knitting an authentic sense of community. While it was easy to listen to like-minded people, it was much harder to sit still when ideas differed or were at odds with what we thought was best. In *Finding Sanctuary* (2006), Abbot Christopher Jamison writes about how good conversation is implicit in the vow of *conversatio morum*. For Benedict, community meant that every person's contribution to common life was welcome even when it might be difficult to accept. The greatest obstacles to true community were murmuring and grumbling (Rule of St. Benedict 40:9) for as Abbot Christopher notes, "Grumbling is the opposite of good conversation; it is the denial of the vow of *conversatio morum* and so is prohibited in the strongest terms."[9]

A good conversation keeps us from falling into patterns that erode community and breed a spirit of complaint, suspicion, and disregard for what others have to offer. Rather, genuine conversation reveals our strengths and our vulnerabilities, letting people know that their opinions really matter.

Whose voices do you resist as sources of knowledge and inspiration? Why?

[9] Christopher Jamison, O.S.B., *Finding Sanctuary: Monastic Steps for Everyday Life* (Collegeville, MN: Liturgical Press, 2006), 127.

CONTRIBUTORS

Virginia Stillwell (*Hospitality*) is director of liturgy and worship at St. John Neumann Parish in Eagan, Minnesota.

Rachel Mark (*Community*) is director of religious education at St. Thomas More Parish in Brookings, South Dakota.

Mark McCormick (*Listening*) is pastor of Our Lady of the Black Hills Parish in Piedmont, South Dakota.

Steve Meyer (*Reverence for All People*) is a deacon at St. Elizabeth Ann Seton Parish in Green Bay, Wisconsin, and president of The Karma Group, a marketing firm.

Kathy Langer (*Justice*) is director of social concerns for Catholic Charities in St. Cloud, Minnesota.

Rodney Bluml (*Stewardship*) is pastoral associate at St. Joseph Parish in Marion, Iowa.

Barbara Sutton (*Conversatio*) is director of ministerial formation and field education at the School of Theology, Saint John's University.

Victor Klimoski (*Editor*) is director of lifelong learning for the School of Theology, Saint John's University.